nearly impossible
BRAIN
BAFFLERS

Official
American Mensa
puzzle book

TIM SOLE &
ROD MARSHALL

Sterling Publishing Co., Inc.
New York

Dedication

Because they were

$$\begin{array}{r} 2 \text{ good} \\ 2 \text{ us} \\ 2 \text{ be} \\ \underline{4} \text{ got} \\ 10 \end{array}$$

this book is dedicated to our families, who have accepted with remarkable patience our fascination with puzzles. To Liz, Heather, and Lynsey Marshall, and Judy, David, Zoe, and Catherine Sole. We hope you will be pleased with the prospect of seeing more of us again, and we hope you enjoy this book.

Edited by Peter Gordon

Library of Congress Cataloging-in-Publication Data Available

10 9 8 7 6 5 4 3 2 1

Published by Sterling Publishing Company, Inc.
387 Park Avenue South, New York, N.Y. 10016
© 1998 by Tim Sole & Rod Marshall
Distributed in Canada by Sterling Publishing
‰ Canadian Manda Group, One Atlantic Avenue, Suite 105
Toronto, Ontario, Canada M6K 3E7
Distributed in Great Britain and Europe by Cassell PLC
Wellington House, 125 Strand, London WC2R 0BB, England
Distributed in Australia by Capricorn Link (Australia) Pty Ltd.
P.O. Box 6651, Baulkham Hills, Business Centre, NSW 2153, Australia

Manufactured in the United States of America
All rights reserved

Sterling ISBN 0-8069-6293-3

Contents

PUZZLES

1. What word, expression, or name is depicted below?

FAREDCE

Answer, page 69

2. Find a ten-digit number containing each digit once, so that the number formed by the first n digits is divisible by n for each value of n between 1 and 10.

Answer, page 63

3. When the examination results were published, one college found that all 32 of its students were successful in at least one of the three exams that each of them had taken. Of the students who did not pass Exam One, the number who passed Exam Two was exactly half of the number who passed Exam Three. The number who passed only Exam One was the same as the number who passed only one of the other two exams, and three more than the number who passed Exam One and at least one of the other two exams.

How many students passed more than one exam?

Answer, page 65

4. If 89 players enter a single elimination tennis tournament, how many matches would it take to decide the winner, excluding byes?

Answer, page 91

5. Using exactly two 2s and any of the standard mathematical symbols, write down an expression whose value is five.

Answer, page 65

6. What word, expression, or name is depicted below?

Answer, page 88

7. This puzzle was devised by Dr. Karl Fabel and published in 1949 in "T.R.D.'s Diamond Jubilee" issue of the *Fairy Chess Review.*

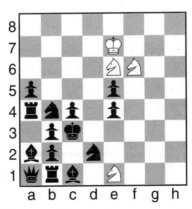

White to play and mate in sixty.

Answer, page 68

8. What word, expression, or name is depicted below?

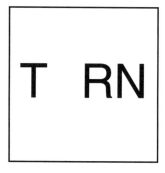

Answer, page 67

9. Find a ten-digit number whose first digit is the number of ones in the number, whose second digit is the number of twos in the number, whose third digit is the number of threes in the number, and so on up to the tenth digit, which is the number of zeros in the number.

Answer, page 77

10. Without using a calculator, guess which is bigger: e^π or π^e?

Answer, page 90

11. A selection of eight cards is dealt with every second card being returned to the bottom of the pack. Thus the top card goes to the table, card two goes to the bottom of the pack, card three goes to the table, card four to the bottom of the pack, and so on. This procedure continues until all the cards are dealt.

The order in which the cards appear on the table is:

A K A K A K A K

How were the cards originally stacked?

Answer, page 65

12. Gambler A chooses a series of three possible outcomes from successive throws of a die, depending simply on whether the number thrown each time is odd (O) or even (E). Gambler B then chooses a different series of three successive possible outcomes. The die is then thrown as often as necessary until either gambler's chosen series of outcomes occurs.

For example, Gambler A might choose the series EOE and B might choose OEE. If successive throws gave, say, EEOOEOE, then A would win the game after the seventh throw. Had the sixth throw been E rather than O, then B would have won.

A has chosen the series EEE and B, who was thinking of choosing OEE, changes his mind to OOO. Has B reduced his chance of winning the game or is it still the same?

Answer, page 91

13. What word, expression, or name is depicted below?

Answer, page 76

14. Find three different two-digit primes where the average of any two is a prime, and the average of all three is a prime.

Answer, page 81

15. Each letter in the sum below represents a different digit. Can you crack the code and discover the uncoded sum?

T	W	E	L	V	E
T	W	E	L	V	E
T	W	E	L	V	E
T	W	E	L	V	E
T	W	E	L	V	E
+ T	H	I	R	T	Y
N	I	N	E	T	Y

Answer, page 86

16. A spider is in a rectangular warehouse measuring 40 × 10 × 10 meters. The spider is on the 10-by-10-meter wall, 5 meters from the sides and 1 meter above the ground. The proverbial fly is on the opposite wall 5 meters from the sides and 1 meter below the ceiling. What is the shortest route for the spider to walk to the fly?

Answer, page 92

17. What word, expression, or name is depicted below?

Answer, page 71

18. In a game of table tennis, 24 of the 37 points played were won by the player serving, and Smith beat Jones 21-16. Remembering in table tennis that service alternates every five points, who served first?

Answer, page 63

19. This chess puzzle by C.S. Kipping was published in the *Manchester City News* in 1911.

White to play and mate in three.

Answer, page 64

20. What word, expression, or name is depicted below?

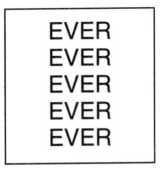

Answer, page 71

21. In the three envelopes shown, the statements on one of the three are both true, the statements on another are both false, and the remaining envelope has one statement that is true and one that is false.

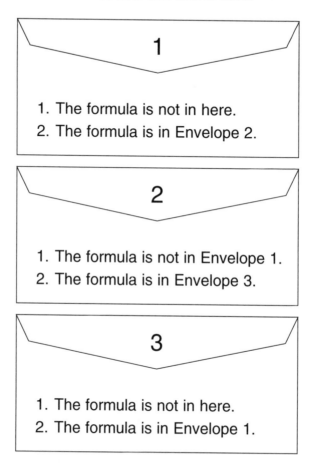

1

1. The formula is not in here.
2. The formula is in Envelope 2.

2

1. The formula is not in Envelope 1.
2. The formula is in Envelope 3.

3

1. The formula is not in here.
2. The formula is in Envelope 1.

Which envelope contains the formula?

Answer, page 63

22. How can eleven matches make nine, nine matches make ten, and ten matches make five?

Answer, page 89

23. Caesar and Brutus are playing a game in which each says the next number from a well-known sequence. The first 20 terms of the sequence are given below:

1 2 3 2 1 2 3 4 2 1 2 3 4 3 2 3 4 5 3 2

The fortieth term is 2. If Caesar began the game, who will be the first to say 10?

Answer, page 65

24. This (okay, somewhat misshapen) Valentine heart consists of one large semicircle beneath two smaller semicircles. The arrow passes right through the point at which the two smaller semicircles meet.

Which part of the heart's perimeter is the longer: that lying above the line of the arrow, or that lying below?

Answer, page 75

25. What word, expression, or name is depicted below?

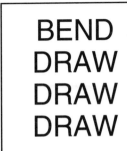

BEND
DRAW
DRAW
DRAW

Answer, page 80

26. This week's chart of the top 40 pop songs has just been published. The song that was at number 35 in last week's chart has dropped out, and there is a new entry at number 32. There are also five non-movers, at positions 1, 23, 29, 31 and 37. Of the other 34 songs in the new chart, 18 have moved up and 16 down, but in every instance the number of positions moved, whether up or down, was a factor (greater than one, but possibly equal to the number itself) of the song's position in last week's chart.

The titles of last week's top 40 are shown below. Complete this week's chart.

Last week		This week	Last week		This week
Atomic	1	Atomic	Valentine	21	
Blockbuster	2		What	22	
Classic	3		Xanadu	23	Xanadu
Dizzy	4		YMCA	24	
Emma	5		Zabadak!	25	
Footloose	6		Autumn Almanac	26	
Gaye	7		Angie Baby	27	
Hello	8		Another Day	28	
Intuition	9		Angel Eyes	29	Angel Eyes
Jesamine	10		Angel Fingers	30	
Kayleigh	11		Amateur Hour	31	Amateur Hour
Lamplight	12		Angela Jones	32	New entry
Mickey	13		Ain't Nobody	33	
Night	14		American Pie	34	
Obsession	15		Ant Rap	35	
Perfect	16		Alphabet Street	36	
Question	17		Alternate Title	37	Alternate Title
Reward	18		As Usual	38	
Sandy	19		Adoration Waltz	39	
True	20		Always Yours	40	

Answer, page 87

27. What word, expression, or name is depicted below?

Answer, page 63

28. The following was originally a list of five-letter words, but in each case two consecutive letters (though never the first two) have been removed. The 26 missing letters are all different. What was the original list?

A	N	T
A	S	S
B	A	Y
C	O	Y
D	I	M
E	E	L
F	A	R
M	A	R
P	I	E
S	E	E
T	I	E
T	O	P
W	I	N

Answer, page 62

29. There is one in a minute and two in a moment, but only one in a million years. What are we talking about?

Answer, page 93

30. Find nine different integers from 1 to 20 inclusive such that no combination of any three of the nine integers form an arithmetic progression. For example, if two of the integers chosen were 7 and 13, then that would preclude 1, 10, and 19 from being included.

Answer, page 67

31. This puzzle was composed by Hans August and Dr. Karl Fabel, and was published in 1949 in *Romana de Sah.*

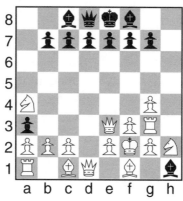

White has just made his seventeenth move.
What was Black's ninth move, and what
were the moves that followed it?

Answer, page 90

32. Two travelers set out at the same time to travel opposite ways round a circular railway. Trains start each way every 15 minutes, on the hour, 15 minutes past, half past, and 45 minutes past. Clockwise trains take two hours for the journey, counterclockwise trains take three hours. Including trains seen at the starting point and the ones they are traveling on, how many trains did each traveler see on his journey?

Answer, page 81

33. The Roman numerals still in use are I = 1, V = 5, X = 10, L = 50, C = 100, D = 500, and M = 1000. Examples of four Roman numbers are VIII = 8, LXXVI = 76, CXXXVI = 136, and MDCCCLXII = 1862.

Today, the Roman numbers IIII, VIIII, and DCCCC are usually abbreviated as IV, IX, and CM, respectively, a numeral to the left of a higher numeral denoting subtraction. Where there is an opportunity, these abbreviations are used in this cross-number, together with CD for CCCC, XC for LXXXX, and XL for XXXX. Thus 1904 would be written as MCMIV and 49 as XLIX. Note that the logical extension of this method of abbreviation, such as IL for 49, for example, was never fully developed and so is not used here. All that is used, where there is an opportunity, are the six usual abbreviations already mentioned.

In the grid below all answers are Roman numerals and, when converted to Arabic (normal) numbers, are palindromes (none starting with zero) of two digits or more. One number occurs twice, the rest are all different.

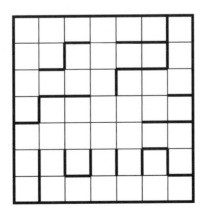

Answer, page 86

34. We place in a box 13 white marbles and 15 black. We also have 28 black marbles outside the box.

We remove two marbles from the box. If they have a different color, we put the white one back in the box. If they have the same color, we put a black marble in the box. We continue doing this until only one marble is left in the box. What is its color?

Answer, page 74

35. What word, expression, or name is depicted below?

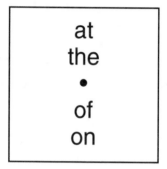

Answer, page 70

36. A drawer contains a number of red and blue socks. If I pull two out at random, then the chance of them being a red pair is a half and the chance of them being a blue pair is a twelfth. How many socks are in the drawer?

Answer, page 81

37. A long time ago, you could buy eight hens for a dollar or one sheep for a dollar, and cows were ten dollars each. A farmer buying animals of each type bought a hundred animals for a hundred dollars. What animals did he buy?

Answer, page 83

38. What word, expression, or name is depicted below?

Answer, page 71

39. Are 1997 nickels worth more than 1992 nickels?
Answer, page 73

40. Insert the missing letter:

J ? M A M J J A
Answer, page 72

41. In a league of four soccer teams, each team played the other three teams. Two points were awarded for a win and one point for a tie. After all six games were played, a final league table was prepared, as shown below:

Team	Won	Tied	Lost	Goals for	Goals against	Points
A	3	0	0	6	1	6
B	1	1	1	2	4	3
C	1	0	2	2	2	2
D	0	1	2	2	5	1

What was the score in each of the six games?
Answer, page 78

42. Lynsey is a biology student. Her project for this term is measuring the effect of an increase in vitamin C in the diet of 25 laboratory mice. Each mouse will have a different diet supplement of between 1 to 50 units. Fractions of a unit are not possible.

Although the university pays for the mice's food, Lynsey has to buy the vitamin C supplement herself. The first consideration in designing this experiment was therefore to minimize the total number of supplements.

The second consideration was that no mouse should have an exact multiple of another mouse's supplement. Thus, if one mouse was on a supplement of 14 units, then this would preclude supplements of 1, 2, 7, 28, and 42 units.

What supplements should Lynsey use?

Answer, page 69

43. Find two ten-digit numbers, each containing the digits from 0 to 9 once and once only, with the property that successive pairs of digits, from left to right, are divisible in turn by 2, 3, 4, 5, 6, 7, 8, 9, and 10.

Answer, page 72

44. What word, expression, or name is depicted below?

Answer, page 76

45. What are the numbers in the tenth line of the following pyramid?

```
            1
           1 1
           2 1
          1 2 1 1
        1 1 1 2 2 1
        3 1 2 2 1 1
      1 3 1 1 2 2 2 1
    1 1 1 3 2 1 3 2 1 1
  3 1 1 3 1 2 1 1 1 3 1 2 2 1
```

Answer, page 71

46. What word, expression, or name is depicted below?

Answer, page 76

47. What digit does each letter represent in the multiplication below, given that no two letters stand for the same digit?

$$
\begin{array}{r}
\text{LAGER} \\
\times\ 4 \\
\hline
\text{REGAL}
\end{array}
$$

Answer, page 74

48. The order of the clues has been muddled up, but 21-Across is correct.

Answer, page 84

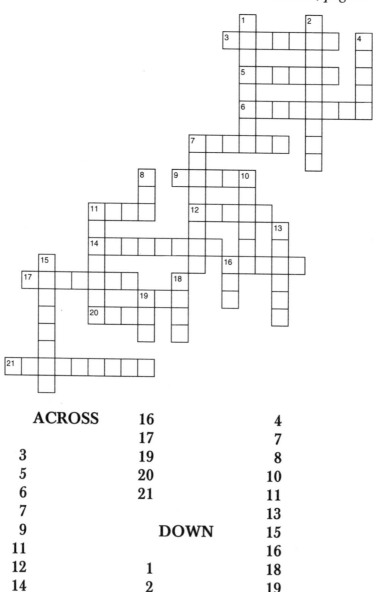

	ACROSS	16	4
		17	7
	3	19	8
	5	20	10
	6	21	11
	7		13
	9	DOWN	15
	11		16
	12	1	18
	14	2	19

49. What word, expression, or name is depicted below?

Answer, page 82

50. Letters other than "x" each represent a different digit. An "x," however, may represent any digit. There is no remainder. Find which digits the letters and each "x" stand for:

```
                O  N  E
  T  R  Y )  T  H  I  S  x
             x  x  x
                x  x  x
                x  x  x
                x  x  x  x
                x  x  x  x
```

Answer, page 93

51. The number 6 has factors (not counting itself) of 1, 2, and 3, which add up to 6. The number 28 has the same property, since its factors, 1, 2, 4, 7, and 14, add up to 28. What four-digit number has this property?

Answer, page 73

52. Between noon and midnight, but not counting these times, how often will the minute hand and hour hand of a clock overlap?

Answer, page 69

53. What word, expression, or name is depicted below?

Answer, page 91

54. A set of building blocks contains a number of wooden cubes. The six faces of each cube are painted, each with a single color, in such a way that no two adjacent faces have the same color. Given that only five different colors have been used and that no two of the blocks are identical in their colorings, what is the maximum number of blocks there can be in the set?

Answer, page 64

55. The Bowls Club has fewer than 100 members. To the nearest whole number, 28% of the members are former committee members, 29% are current committee members, and 42% have never been on the committee. Again to the nearest whole number, 35% of the former committee members are women. What is the total membership of the club?

Answer, page 66

56. The pars for a nine-hole golf course designed by a mathematician are:

     3 3 5 4 4 3 5 5 4

On which very well-known series (as well-known as one, two, three, etc.) are the pars based?

Answer, page 71

57. This may seem self-contradictory, but find three integers in arithmetic progression (that is, with equal differences, such as 230, 236, and 242) whose product is prime.

Answer, page 86

58. What is the next term in this series:

     1248   1632   6412   8256   ?

Answer, page 69

59. What word, expression, or name is depicted below?

Answer, page 67

60. The ages of Old and Young total 48. Old is twice as old as Young was when Old was half as old as Young will be when Young is three times as old as Old was when Old was three times as old as Young. How old is Old?

Answer, page 76

61. Consider a five-by-five version of a chessboard with one player having five queens and the other player three queens. There are no other pieces. Can you place the queens on the board so that neither player's queens can capture one of his or her opponent's queens?

Answer, page 83

62.

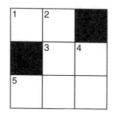

ACROSS

1 Starting piece between 3 and 4
3 2-Down minus a perfect square
5 Three!

DOWN

2 A perfect square
4 1.5 times 5-Across (or two-thirds of 5-Across)

Answer, page 63

63. What word, expression, or name is depicted below?

NE14
10S?

Answer, page 74

64. A full set of dominoes (0-0 to 6-6) has been laid out in a rectangular array. The numbers in the diagram represent the spots on the dominoes, and the puzzle is to identify the position of each domino within the pattern.

```
1 2 6 1 6 3 4 5
3 3 6 4 3 2 5 4
3 0 6 0 3 1 2 2
0 5 5 4 6 5 0 2
0 2 5 1 5 0 0 1
6 4 3 4 4 1 1 1
2 2 6 4 5 0 3 6
```

Answer, page 86

65. At the end of the soccer season, every player had scored a prime number of goals and the average for the eleven players was also a prime number. No player's tally was the same as anyone else's, and neither was it the same as the average.

Given that nobody had scored more than 45 goals, how many goals did each player score?

Answer, page 74

66. What word, expression, or name is depicted below?

Answer, page 72

67. Allwyn, Aitkins, and Arthur are to fight a three-way duel. The order in which they shoot will be determined by lot and they will continue to shoot until two are dead. Allwyn never misses, Aitkins is eighty percent accurate, and Arthur, the cleverest of the three, hits his target just half of the time. Who has the best chance of surviving?

Answer, page 79

68. What word, expression, or name is depicted below?

Answer, page 81

69. Can you subdivide a square measuring eleven by eleven into five rectangles such that the five lengths and five widths of the rectangles are all different and integral? There are two solutions.

Answer, page 83

70. What are the missing numbers?
> 31   62   __   25   56   __   19

Answer, page 84

71. Find three different positive integers whose factorials are each one less than a perfect square, and whose factorials sum to a perfect square.

Answer, page 73

72. I recently overheard a conversation that went roughly as follows:

Bob: "Here's a problem that might interest you. On my bus this morning there were only three other passengers, all of whom I knew. We discovered that the product of their ages was 2,450, and that the sum was exactly twice your age. How old are they?"

Jim: "Hang on. You haven't given me enough info."

Bob: "Oh, sorry. I forgot to mention that one of the passengers on the bus was someone older than me, and I am—"

Jim: "I know how old you are. And I now know the passengers' ages, too."

How old are Jim, Bob, and each of the three other passengers?

Answer, page 79

73. This puzzle is based on a theme by W.A. Shinkman, and the mate-in-three was first solved by Sam Loyd. The puzzle below was published in the *Leeds Mercury Supplement* in 1895.

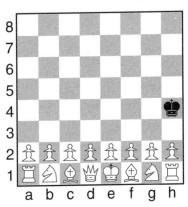

White to play and mate in three.

Answer, page 88

74. Construct a game that will leave the position shown for Puzzle 73 after Black's sixteenth move.

Answer, page 89

75. In a game of poker, one of the hands of five cards had the following features:
• There was no card above a 10 (an ace is above a 10 in poker).
• No two cards were of the same value.
• All four suits were represented.
• The total values of the odd and even cards were equal.
• No three cards were in sequence.
• The black cards totaled 10 in value.
• The hearts totaled 14.
• The lowest card was a spade.
    What was the hand?

Answer, page 63

76. What word, expression, or name is depicted below?

```
+-----------+
| D   d   D |
|           |
| d   W   d |
|           |
| D   d   D |
+-----------+
```

Answer, page 88

77. "Bookkeeper" has three consecutive double letters. What common two-word phrase, if you remove the space, also has three consecutive double letters?

Answer, page 74

78. What word, expression, or name is depicted below?

Answer, page 65

79. Divide the following figure into four identical parts, with each part made up of whole squares only. Each of the four parts should also contain one O and one X, but not necessarily in the same relative positions.

O			X		
			X		
		O			
	X		X		
			O	O	

Answer, page 81

80. Using each of the numbers 1, 5, 6, and 7 once and once only, parentheses as required, and any combination and any number of the following symbols:

$$+ \quad - \quad \times \quad /$$

find an expression that equals 21.

Answer, page 82

81. P and Q are integers that between them contain each of the digits from 0 to 9 once and once only. What is the maximum value of P × Q?

Answer, page 69

82. What word, expression, or name is depicted below?

Answer, page 72

83. A total of five triangles can be seen in the diagram on the left.

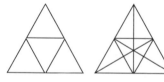

How many triangles can be found in the diagram on the right?

Answer, page 76

84. Using just four sixes, parentheses where necessary, and the following seven symbols as needed:

$$+ \quad - \quad \times \quad / \quad . \quad ! \quad \sqrt{}$$

find an expression for 29.

Answer, page 80

85. What word, expression, or name is depicted below?

Answer, page 79

86. In this long division, each "x" represents a digit. Find which digits each "x" stands for:

```
            x x . x x x
    x x ) x x x x
          x x
          x x x
          x x
            x x
            x x
            x x x
            x x x
              x x
              x x
```

Answer, page 80

87. What are the two missing numbers in the series below?

_ _ 3 3 7 7 2 3 6 5

Answer, page 74

88. Five soccer teams, United, County, Rovers, Albion, and Thistle, took part in a league tournament. Their colors were white, yellow, green, red, and blue, though not necessarily in that order. No teams were tied in the standings at the end of the tournament. From the following information, determine for each team its captain, colors, and position in which it finished in the league.

• Rovers did not win the league, but finished higher than fourth.

• Neither Albion nor the team in green finished in the top three.

• Evans captained the team in yellow.

• Cooke's team finished ahead of County, which was captained by Dixon.

• Allen's team finished second and Boyle's team finished last.

• The team in white finished lower than both United and the team in blue, but above Evans's team.

• Albion was not the green team and United was not the blue team.

Answer, page 62

89. What word, expression, or name is depicted below?

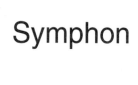

Answer, page 83

90. Arrange the digits from 1 to 9 in a 3 × 3 array in such a way that the sum of a number's immediate neighbors (including diagonals) is a multiple of that number.

9	5	1
6	7	2
4	3	8

The example shows an unsatisfactory attempt. The three numbers bordering 9 add to 18, which is a multiple of 9 as required, and the numbers bordering 1, 2, 3, 4, and 5 also meet the condition specified. The numbers bordering 6, 7, and 8, however, do not meet the required condition.

Answer, page 74

91. What word, expression, or name is depicted below?

GIVE GET
GIVE GET
GIVE GET
GIVE GET

Answer, page 62

92. What is the minimum difference between two integers that between them contain each digit once?

Answer, page 63

93. This position was created by F. Amelung and published in *Düna Zeitung* in 1897. It is a puzzle that has since defeated many good chess players, and one cannot but wonder whether it has ever occurred naturally in a real game. If it did, and you were White and about to play, how could you force mate in two?

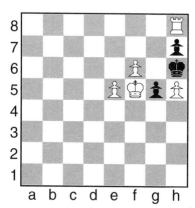

White to play and mate in two.

Answer, page 79

94. Arrange the digits from one to nine in a three by three square in such a way that each of the three-digit numbers reading across, and the three-digit number on the diagonal from top left to bottom right, are all perfect squares.

Answer, page 88

95. The digital root of a number is obtained by summing its digits and then repeating this process until the answer is a single digit. For example, the digital root of 8777 is 2.

Noting that any number divisible by nine has a digital root of nine, what is the digital root of $(9^{6130} + 2)^{4875}$?

Answer, page 91

96. If six equilateral triangles each of unit area are joined edge-to-edge, twelve different shapes each of six units in area can be constructed as shown below:

Show that it is impossible to form any six of these shapes into a six-by-six-by-six equilateral triangle of 36 units in area.

Answer, page 66

97. Which of the following poker hands is stronger?

A♣ A♦ A♥ K♣ K♥
or
A♣ A♥ K♣ K♦ K♠

Think about it!

Answer, page 82

98. Continue the sequence:

202 122 232 425 262 728 ? ?

Answer, page 65

99. What word, expression, or name is depicted below?

Answer, page 89

100. The third and fourth powers of this integer contain between them exactly one of each digit. What is the integer?

Answer, page 80

101. Complete the eight words using each letter of the alphabet once and once only.

```
_ A _ E R I _ _
_ U _ _ _ E
_ I _ _ E
_ _ L _ E R
_ I _ _
_ _ A P
B R _ _ _ N
_ O L _ _ A _
```

Answer, page 76

102.   *Is the tenth root of ten*
               A little bit more
            Than the root of the square
              Of the sixth root of four?

Answer, page 62

103. This cross-number uses Roman numbers only and yes, every clue is the same! If you are struggling to remember what the Roman numerals are and how they are used, a description is given in Puzzle 33.

ACROSS

1 A perfect square
7 A perfect square
8 A perfect square
9 A perfect square
10 A perfect square
13 A perfect square
14 A perfect square
17 A perfect square
19 A perfect square
20 A perfect square

DOWN

1 A perfect square
2 A perfect square
3 A perfect square
4 A perfect square
5 A perfect square
6 A perfect square
7 A perfect square
11 A perfect square
12 A perfect square
15 A perfect square
16 A perfect square
18 A perfect square
19 A perfect square

Answer, page 71

104. What word, expression, or name is depicted below?

Answer, page 69

105. A horizontal line from the top of the inside edge of a bicycle tire to the two outside edges of the tire measures 24 centimeters as shown in the side view below:

What is the area of the bicycle tire visible from this view?

Answer, page 73

106. In the following line, cross out six letters so that the remaining letters, without altering their sequence, will spell a familiar English word.

BSAINXLEATNTEARS

Answer, page 63

107. What word, expression, or name is depicted below?

ping**WILLOW**

Answer, page 76

108. What is the smallest integer that can be expressed as the sum of two squares in three different ways? The answer is less than 500.

Answer, page 73

109. Two right triangles share the same hypotenuse AB. The shorter sides of the first triangle are 13 and 18 units; the shorter sides of the second are 7 and 20 units.

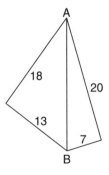

Clearly we are not measuring in base ten. What base is being used, and how long is the hypotenuse?

Answer, page 85

110. A ball with a diameter of 40 centimeters is lying on the ground, tight against a wall:

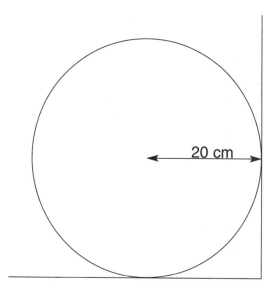

Can a ball with a diameter of seven centimeters pass through the gap between the ball, ground, and wall?

Answer, page 70

111. What word, expression, or name is depicted below?

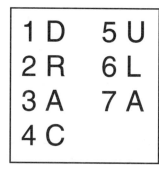

Answer, page 71

112. What word, expression, or name is depicted below?

wear
long

Answer, page 65

113. This puzzle by Sam Loyd was published in the *Holyoke Transcript* in 1876.

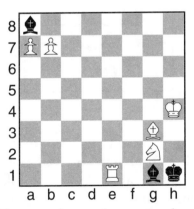

White to play and mate in three.

Answer, page 77

114. "Strength" is an eight-letter word with only one vowel. What's an eight-letter word with five vowels in a row?

Answer, page 82

115. The array of blocks shown below spells the word "PUZZLE." Could we be looking at six different views of the same block, or is one or more of the views inconsistent with the others?

Answer, page 81

116. What word, expression, or name is depicted below?

Answer, page 87

117. Using the digits one to nine in ascending order and no more than three standard arithmetical signs, find an expression that equals 100. An example that uses six standard arithmetical signs is shown below:

$$1 + (2 \times 3) - 4 + (56 \div 7) + 89 = 100$$

Answer, page 83

118. If the integers that contain each digit once were arranged in ascending order, which would be the millionth? (Numbers can't start with 0.)

Answer, page 76

119. A Christmas decoration comprises a symmetrical four-pointed star supported by three threads. The decoration hangs in the center of a small circular window:

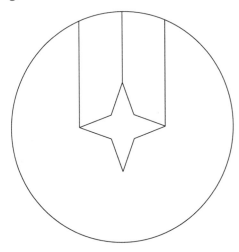

The central thread is 4 centimeters long, and the outer two are each 6 centimeters long. What is the width of the star?

Answer, page 85

120. What word, expression, or name is depicted below?

79 S 34 A 92

F 185 E 376

7 T 27 Y 12

Answer, page 69

121. Without using a calculator, determine which is greater: $3\frac{1}{8} \times 3\frac{1}{5}$ or $3 \times \sqrt[3]{37}$?

Answer, page 70

122. In the expression below, do the three letters represent three different digits?

$$(\textbf{ANNE})_{\text{base 8}} - (\textbf{ANNE})_{\text{base 5}} = (\textbf{ANNE})_{\text{base 7}}$$

Answer, page 72

123. Eric the Halibut is swimming to the right. Move three sticks (and his eye, smile, and bubbles) so that he is swimming to the left.

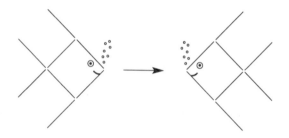

Answer, page 87

124. What word, expression, or name is depicted below?

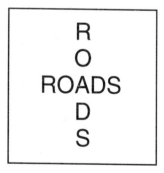

Answer, page 88

125. Losers' Chess is a fun game that often turns in a surprise result. To play it, ignore checks and checkmates, for the object is either to lose all of one's men, king included, or be stalemated (unable to play a move). Players must capture an opponent's man if they can, but where there is a choice, can choose which. All other rules are the same as for ordinary chess.

Puzzles in Losers' Chess are rare, and ones with an unusual twist like the one below even rarer. This one, by T.R. Dawson, was first published in 1925 in *Das Wochenschach.* In the first analysis it looks like Black can force White to stalemate him, but White, who is playing up the board, can play and win by forcing Black to cause the stalemate. How?

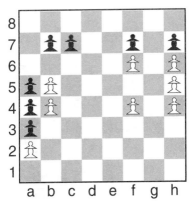

White to play and win (Losers' Chess rules).

Answer, page 73

126. A ladder 5 meters long leans against a wall. A box measuring 1 × 1 × 1 meters just fits in the gap. If the base of the ladder is nearer to the wall than the top of the ladder is to the ground, how far is the base of the ladder from the wall?

Answer, page 67

127. No answer begins with a zero.

1	2	3	4	5	6	7
8			9			
10			11			12
13		14			15	
16	17		18	19		
20			21			
22					23	

ACROSS

1 See 3-Down
3 A multiple of 3
8 3 × 17-Down
9 2 × 15-Down
10 See 14-Down
11 See 6-Down
13 2 × 4-Down
16 Not 3-Down
18 See 5-Down
20 2 × 2-Down
21 Not 6-Down
22 See 1-Down
23 Same as 20-Down

DOWN

1 2 × 22-Across
2 See 20-Across
3 2 × 1-Across
4 See 13-Across
5 2 × 18-Across
6 3 × 11-Across
7 Same as 23-Across
12 2 × 3-Across
14 2 × 10-Across + 4
15 See 9-Across
17 See 8-Across
19 Square of 23-Across
20 See 23-Across

Answer, page 80

128. What number, when spelled out, has no repeated letters and has each of the vowels (not including Y) once?

Answer, page 82

129. What word, expression, or name is depicted below?

Answer, page 74

130. Shown below are six numbered pool balls arranged in a triangular pattern such that each number in the pattern is equal to the difference between the two numbers above:

Find a similar triangular pattern for fifteen pool balls numbered 1 to 15.

Answer, page 88

131. What is the next term in this series?

      100 121 144 202 244 400 ...

Answer, page 69

132. What are the next two letters in the following series and why?

      W A T N T L I T F S _ _

Answer, page 64

133. The diagram shows a regular pentagram:

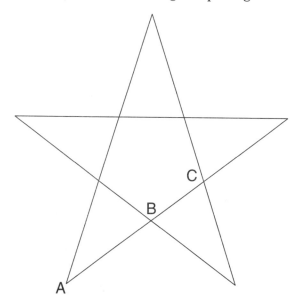

What is the ratio of AB to BC?

Answer, page 78

134.
> *If B is two A,*
> *C three A plus B,*
> *And A is "eleven eleven,"*
> *Is B to the C*
> *Plus C to the B*
> *Divisible by seven?*
>
> *"Eleven eleven,"*
> *So you won't be confused,*
> *Has nothing to do with odd bases.*
> *It's simply ten thou*
> *That's multiplied by*
> *One ninth to four decimal places.*

Answer, page 91

135. Reconstruct the following multiplication, using the digits 2, 3, 5, and 7 only.

```
        x  x  x
           x  x
     _____
     x  x  x  x
  x  x  x  x
  _____
  x  x  x  x  x
```

Answer, page 65

136. What word, expression, or name is depicted below?

Answer, page 88

137. Find a three-digit number containing three different digits where the first digit plus the number formed by the second and third digits, the first digit multiplied by the number formed by the second and third digits, and the sum of the three digits are all perfect squares.

Answer, page 76

138. Which three boys' names are anagrams of one another?

Answer, page 77

139. Five checks by White in four moves (including a double check) followed by a checkmate to solve a puzzle that is more than 500 years old! It was first published by Lucena in 1496.

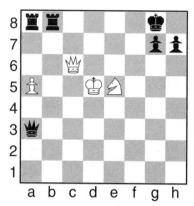

White to play and mate in five.

Answer, page 74

140. Two equal squares, ABCD and DEFG, have the vertex D in common. The angle between the two squares is 60°:

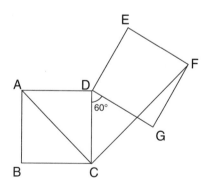

What is the angle ACF?

Answer, page 82

141. Which is bigger?

$$\sqrt{(12 + \sqrt{(12 + \sqrt{(12 + \sqrt{(12 + ...}}}})))$$

or

$$2 + \sqrt{(2 + \sqrt{(2 + \sqrt{(2 + \sqrt{(2 + ...}}}})))$$

Answer, page 83

142. What word, expression, or name is depicted below?

Answer, page 91

143. Find a four-digit number, with four different digits, that is equal to the number formed by its digits in descending order minus the number formed by its digits in ascending order.

Answer, page 66

144. Two candles, one of which was two centimeters longer than the other, were lit for Halloween. The longer and thinner one was lit at 4 P.M. and the shorter but fatter one 15 minutes later. Each candle burned at a steady rate, and by 8 P.M. both were the same length. The thinner one finally burned out at midnight and the fatter one an hour later. How long was each candle originally?

Answer, page 88

145. What word, expression, or name is depicted below?

house
PRAIRIE

Answer, page 66

146. The following eight numbers can be grouped into four pairs such that the higher of each pair divided by the lower is a number (to an average of five decimal places) of particular mathematical significance.

113 323 355 408 577 610 878 987

What are the four pairs?

Answer, page 76

147. The following relationships hold among the ages of the members of a family of four. All ages are integral.

The mother is three times as old as the daughter was when the father was the same age as the mother is now. When the daughter reaches half the age the mother is now, the son will be half as old as the father was when the mother was twice the age the daughter is now. When the father reaches twice the age the mother was when the daughter was the same age as the son is now, the daughter will be four times as old as the son is now. Given that one of their ages is a perfect square, what are the four ages?

Answer, page 83

148. What word, expression, or name is depicted below?

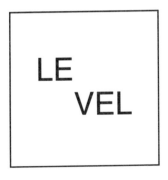

LE
VEL

Answer, page 81

149. Any integer from 1 to 112 inclusive can be expressed with four fours, parentheses where necessary, and use of the following seven symbols as required:

$$+ \quad - \quad \times \quad / \quad . \quad ! \quad \sqrt{}$$

All that is asked for here, however, is an expression for 71. The use of other symbols or nonstandard expressions such as $.(\sqrt{4})$ for 0.2 or $\sqrt{\sqrt{\ldots}}\sqrt{\sqrt{4}}$ for 1 is not permitted.

Answer, page 74

150. *Twice eight are ten of us, and ten but three.*
Three of us are five. What can we be?
If this is not enough, I'll tell you more.
Twelve of us are six, and nine but four.

Answer, page 77

151. In the expression below, each letter represents a different digit:

$$A^5 + B^5 + C^5 + D^5 + E^5 = ABCDE$$

What is ABCDE?

Answer, page 65

152. This self-mate in four was first published by William Shinkman in the *Chess Player's Chronicle* in 1883.

In a fit of kindness, White decides she wants Black to win and offers her resignation. Black turns down White's offer by announcing that he thinks the game should be played to the finish.

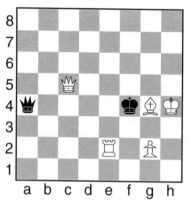

White then forced Black to mate her in four moves anyway. How does White do this?

Answer, page 72

153. What word, expression, or name is depicted below?

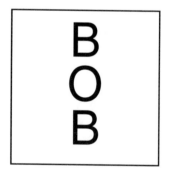

Answer, page 74

154. A professor asked four students how long each of them had been studying. One of the students replied: "We have all been studying a whole number of years, the sum of our years of studying is equal to the number of years you have been teaching, and the product of our years of studying is 180."

"I'm sorry," replied the professor after some thought, "but that doesn't give me enough information."

"Yes, you're right," agreed another of the students. "But if we told you whether any of us were into double figures in our years of study, then you could answer your question."

How long had each of the four been studying?

Answer, page 62

155. In how many different ways can the 16 chess pieces be arranged on one side of a chess board for the start of a game of chess? For example, the two rooks can switch places, and any two of the eight pawns can be swapped and still leave the standard starting position.

Answer, page 86

156. What word, expression, or name is depicted below?

Answer, page 75

157. In an athletics contest between the army, the navy, and the air force, each team entered three athletes in a particular race. The winning athlete scored eight points, the runner-up seven, third place six, and so on down to none for last place.

Once the race was run, the judges needed a photograph to separate the first two army men to finish. A member of the navy's team finished last. When the points were totaled, all three teams were found to have the same score.

Find by team the order in which the nine athletes finished.

Answer, page 71

158. What word, expression, or name is depicted below?

Answer, page 82

159. In a game of chess, Black has agreed to mirror White's first three moves. White promptly mates Black on the fourth move. What were White's moves?

Answer, page 78

160. Which day of the week has an anagram?

Answer, page 70

161. Heather left her hotel room between 7 and 8 P.M. and glanced at her watch. When she next looked at her watch it appeared as if the hour and minute hands had changed places. In fact, it was now between 10 and 11 P.M. Exactly how long ago had she left her room?

Answer, page 77

162. One for the children: Would you rather a tiger chased you or a zebra?

Answer, page 85

163. What word, expression, or name is depicted below?

Answer, page 80

164. Find a three-by-three magic square in which the following properties are true:
• The sum of each row, column, and long diagonal is 111.
• Each cell has a number with no factors other than one and itself.
• Each cell is different.
    As a hint, you should start by figuring out the center square.

Answer, page 67

165. Both my father and my father's grandfather were born in years that can be expressed as $m^n - n^m$, where m and n are both integers. In which years were they born?

Answer, page 66

166. What word, expression, or name is depicted below?

Answer, page 78

ANSWERS

88.

Position	Team	Captain	Color
1	United	Cooke	Red
2	Rovers	Allen	Blue
3	County	Dixon	White
4	Albion	Evans	Yellow
5	Thistle	Boyle	Green

154. Of all possible sets of four whole numbers whose product is 180, the only sets with sums that are not unique are those with sums of 18 and 22. Thus the professor must have been teaching for one of those two periods.

If it is 18 years, then the four lengths of study could be 1, 5, 6, and 6 years; 2, 2, 5, and 9 years; or 2, 3, 3, and 10 years. If it is 22 years, then the possible combinations are 1, 2, 9, and 10 years, or 2, 2, 3, and 15 years.

We are told that knowing whether any of the students were into double figures would enable the professor to determine the four periods, so a length of teaching of 22 years is ruled out. Of the three sets whose sum is 18 years, two contain no double-digit numbers, which leaves the third set as the only possibility.

Thus the four students had been studying for 2, 3, 3, and 10 years.

91. Forgive and forget.

28. ANGST, ABYSS, BAWDY, COMFY, DENIM, EXPEL, FAKIR, MAJOR, PIQUE, SERVE, TITLE, TOPAZ, WINCH.

102. The verse asks whether $10^{1/10} > 2^{1/3}$ or, if we raise each side to the power of 30, whether $10^3 > 2^{10}$? The answer is "no."

62. Five across is three factorial, which is SIX. Two-thirds of SIX or, more precisely, the last two-thirds of the word SIX, is IX, which is the Roman numeral nine.

P	I	
	2	I
S	I	X

106. By crossing out "SIX LETTERS," we are left with the word "BANANA."

18. Smith served first. One possible proof is as follows:
Whoever served first would have served on 20 of the points played and the other player would have served on 17 of them. Suppose the first player won x of the points on which he served and y of the points served by his opponent. The total number of points lost by the player who served them is then $20 - x + y$. This must equal 13, since we are told that 24 of the 37 points were won by the player serving. Thus $x = 7 + y$, and the first server won $(7 + y) + y = 7 + 2y$ points in total. This is an odd number, and only Smith won an odd number of points. Thus Smith served first.

27. Mixed bag.

92. $50,123 - 49,876 = 247$.

75. ♠2, ♥9, ♥5, ♦4, ♣8.

2. 3,816,547,290.

21. The envelope with the formula is Envelope 3.

54. The maximum number of blocks in the set is 55.

If only three of the five available colors are used, then opposite faces of a block must have the same color. Thus by symmetry there is only one way in which a block can be painted with any three given colors, and there are 10 different ways in which three colors can be chosen.

If four colors are used, then two pairs of opposite faces must each have the same color. By symmetry it doesn't matter which way around the other two faces are painted. The colors for the two pairs of matching faces can be chosen in ten different ways, and the other two colors can then be chosen in three ways, giving an overall total of 30 combinations.

Finally, if five colors are used then just one pair of opposite faces will have the same color. The remaining four colors can be arranged in three different ways, so using five colors gives a total of $5 \times 3 = 15$ combinations.

The maximum number of blocks in the set is therefore $10 + 30 + 15 = 55$.

19. White's key move of **1 Ka5!!** seems self-destructive and a sure provocation for Black to play **1 ... e1(Q)+**. White's reply, **2 Kb6!**, seems even more provocative as it offers Black no fewer than seven different moves with which to check White's king. Each one, however, can be defended by moving the knight at c6 for a discovered checkmate. If Black moves **1 ... Rg7** then **2 Ne7+ Ka7 3 Nc8** mate. If **1 ... Rg5** then **2 Kb6** (threatening **3 Ne7** mate) Rxd5 **3 Nc7** mate. If **1 ... Kb7** then **2 Ne7+ Ka7 3 Nc8** mate.

132. The letters are the first letters of the words in the question. Thus the next two letters are A and W.

151. ABCDE is 93084.

5. $\sqrt{.2^{-2}}$, which shows that two twos can make five!

112. Long underwear.

78. On the double.

11. AAKAAKKK.

3. Eleven students passed Exam One only, three passed Exam Two only, and eight passed Exam Three only. Thus ten students passed more than one exam.

98. Regrouping the sequence as 20, 21, 22, 23, 24, 25, 26, 27, 28, it is obvious the next three terms in this more normal format are 29, 30, and 31. Using the question's format, the required answer is 293 and 031.

135.

		7	7	5
			3	3
	2	3	2	5
2	3	2	5	
2	5	5	7	5

23. The series is generated by counting the number of characters in the corresponding Roman numeral, as shown for the first ten numbers below:

I	II	III	IV	V	VI	VII	VIII	IX	X
1	2	3	2	1	2	3	4	2	1

The first term to equal 10 is the 288th in the series: CCLXXXVIII. Thus the answer to the question is Brutus.

145. *Little House on the Prairie.*

143. 6174.

55. There are 26 former committee members (9 of whom are women), 27 committee members, and 39 members who have never been on the committee. This gives a total of 92 members.

96. To prove this, color the large triangle of 36 units in area as shown, giving 21 light and 15 dark unit triangles.

If the twelve available shapes are colored in a similar manner, ten are found to have an equal number of light and dark unit triangles. In the remaining two cases, there are four light and two dark (or vice versa). However, to tile the shape above requires at least three pieces where the difference between the numbers of light and dark triangles is two. Since there are only two such pieces, no solution is possible.

165. My father was born in 1927 ($2^{11} - 11^2$), and his grandfather in 1844 ($3^7 - 7^3$).

126. In the diagram below, the two smaller triangles are similar, which means the ratio of their sides is constant and more particularly, that $y/1 = 1/x$.

By the Pythagorean theorem
$(x + 1)^2 + (y + 1)^2 = (x + 1)^2 + (1/x + 1)^2 = 25$ so
$x^4 + 2x^3 + 2x^2 + 2x + 1 = 25x^2$ from which
$(x^2 + x + 1)^2 = 26x^2$ so
$x^2 + (1 - \sqrt{26})x + 1 = 0$ and $x = 0.2605$ meters.

The base of the ladder is 1.2605 meters from the wall.

8. No U-Turn.

59. Cornerstone.

164. The number at the center of any three-by-three magic square is always one-third of the magic square's constant. Thus the center square must be 37. The rest then follows. (Reflected and rotated answers are also possible.)

43	1	67
61	37	13
7	73	31

30. Either 1, 2, 6, 7, 9, 14, 15, 18, 20 or 1, 3, 6, 7, 12, 14, 15, 19, 20.

7. For White to win, he has to force one of Black's knights to move. Then, provided White's king is safe from unwanted checks and White has not moved his own knights, White wins with Ne4 mate or Nd5 mate. The actual winning move will depend upon which knight Black eventually moves.

Black can delay moving a knight for 59 moves! His tactic is to shunt the rook at a4 to and fro to a3 whenever he can. Accordingly, and taking the route that avoids unwanted checks, White uses his king to inhibit the shunting rook by timing the arrival of his king at b5 to follow Black's move Ra3.

On the first four occasions White does this, Black keeps his rook out of danger by moving a pawn on the e file. On the fifth occasion, to avoid moving a knight and to save his rook, Black must block his rook in with a5-a4. On his next move Black is compelled to move a knight and expose himself to an instant checkmate. Note that if Black moves his pawns before he has to, then the mate is simply speeded up. With Black's best defense as shown below, White will mate in sixty.

White's first move can be either Ke8 or Kd6. White's king then proceeds d7, c8, b7, b6, b5. By moving to d7 via e8 or d6, the White king arrives at b5 after an even number of moves. Thus, for move six, Black's shunting rook will be at a3 and Black must move a pawn, lose his rook, or be mated. To defer mate as long as possible, Black must play e4-e3.

After Black's move, e4-e3, White moves his king away from b5 and Black can continue with the shunting of his rook. White must now move his king back to b5 in an odd number of moves in order to catch the shunting rook at a3. The shortest route for White to achieve this that avoids unwanted checks is b6, b7, c8, d7, e8, f8, f7, e8, d7, c8, b7, b6, b5, and this he repeats four times.

On moves 19, 32, and 45 Black takes a break from shunting his rook and moves a pawn on the e file. On move 58, however, Black can do no better than to block his rook in with a5-a4. White then plays a waiting move, Kb6. If Black moves the knight at b4, then White mates with Nd5, and if Black moves the knight at d2, then White mates with Ne4. This gives White mate in sixty.

104. Back and forth.

131. The terms in the series are one hundred in base ten, one hundred in base nine, one hundred in base eight, ..., one hundred in base five. The next term in the series is one hundred in base four, which is 1210.

58. Regrouping the series as 1, 2, 4, 8, 16, 32, 64, 128, and 256, the next two terms in this series are 512 and 1024. The answer to the question is 5121.

42. Supplements to use are: 8, 12, 14, 17, 18, 19, 20, 21, 22, 23, 25, 26, 27, 29, 30, 31, 33, 35, 37, 39, 41, 43, 45, 47, and 49. They total 711.

120. Safety in numbers.

52. Not eleven, but ten times. The times are between 1 and 2, between 2 and 3, and so on, ending with once between 10 and 11. It does not happen between 11 and 12, since it happens at exactly 12 (noon and midnight). The question excludes noon and midnight, so that occurrence doesn't count.

81. $96,420 \times 87,531 = 8,439,739,020$.

1. Red in the face.

110. Let the radius of the largest ball that will fit in the gap be r, and let the distance from the corner to the center of the smaller ball be y.

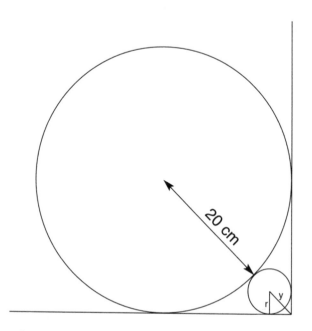

The distance from the corner to the center of the big ball is $20 + r + y = \sqrt{(20^2 + 20^2)}$, so $r + y = \sqrt{800} - 20 = 8.28$ cm. Since $y = \sqrt{(r^2 + r^2)}$, $2r^2 = (8.28 - r)^2$, from which $r^2 + 16.57r - 68.63 = 0$ and $r = 3.43$ cm. This means that the largest ball that can fit in the gap has diameter $2 \times 3.43 = 6.86$ cm, so the answer to the original question is no.

121. $3\frac{1}{8} \times 3\frac{1}{5} = \frac{25}{8} \times \frac{16}{5} = 10$.
$3 \times \sqrt[3]{37} = \sqrt[3]{(27 \times 37)} = \sqrt[3]{999} < \sqrt[3]{1000} = 10$.

160. Monday is an anagram of dynamo.

35. At the point of no return.

45. Each line describes the line above. For example, since line five is 1 1 1 2 2 1, which can be expressed as three ones (3 1), two twos (2 2), and one one (1 1), line six is 3 1 2 2 1 1.

The tenth line in the pyramid is therefore:
1 3 2 1 1 3 1 1 1 2 3 1 1 3 1 1 2 2 1 1.

38. Pin-up.

20. Forever and ever.

157. The positions were first, fifth, and ninth for the navy; second, sixth, and seventh for the air force; and third, fourth, and eighth for the army.

103.

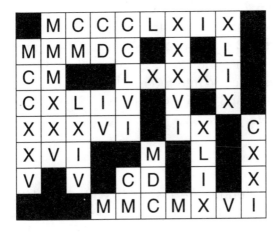

111. Count Dracula.

17. Ambiguous.

56. The series consists of the numbers of letters in the words one, two, three, etc.

122. Rewriting each ANNE in base ten, we have:
$A(8^3 - 5^3 - 7^3) + N(8^2 + 8 - 5^2 - 5 - 7^2 - 7) + E(1 - 1 - 1) = 0$

That is, $44A - 14N - E = 0$. Noting that A, N, and E are all digits of a number written in base five, so A, N, and E are all less than five, $A = 1$, $N = 3$, and $E = 2$ is the unique solution. Thus the three letters do represent three different digits.

40. F for February. The letters are the initials of the first eight months of the year.

152. The key move is **1** Bh3, to which Black must reply with a queen move. If Black plays **1** ... Qa8 or **1** ... Qe8, then **2** Qd4+ Qe4 **3** Qf6+ Qf5 **4** Qg5+ Qxg5 mate.

If Black keeps his queen on the same rank, say **1** ... Qd4, then **2** g3+ Kf3+ **3** Bg4+ Qxg4 mate.

If Black plays any other queen move, then White plays either **2** Qb4+ or **2** Qc4+ or **2** Qd4+ forcing Black to reply with either **2** ... Qxb4 or **2** ... Qxc4 or **2** ... Qxd4 and then White forces Black to win as above. For example, **1** Bh3 Qa6 **2** Qc4+ Qxc4 **3** g3+ Kf3+ **4** Bg4+ Qxg4 mate.

82. Income tax.

43. The solutions are 1,872,549,630 and 7,812,549,630, and are derived as follows: The 5 and 0 can be placed immediately. The sixth digit must be 4. The seventh digit is odd (since every second digit must be even), so it must be 9. The eighth digit must be 6. The ninth digit must be 3. The third digit is 1 or 7, so the fourth digit must be 2. The first three digits are therefore 187 or 781.

66. Split-second timing.

105. Let the radii of the larger and smaller circles be R and r respectively. The desired area is then $\pi R^2 - \pi r^2 = \pi(R^2 - r^2)$.

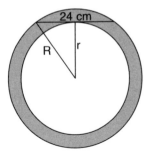

Using the Pythagorean theorem, it can be seen that $R^2 - r^2 = (^{24}\!/_2)^2 = 144$, so the desired area is $144\pi = 452.4$ sq. cm.

39. The value of 1,997 nickels is $99.85, 25 cents more than 1,992 nickels (worth $99.60).

125. Black's last move was a7-a5. It could not have been a6-a5 since a pawn at a6 would have had to capture White's pawn. Neither could it have been b6xa5 since this would imply, given the position of Black's other pawns, that Black had made nine captures (which is impossible since White still has eight pieces on the board). Thus White plays **1** bxa6 e.p.

White wins by being stalemated as follows: **1** … bxa6 **2** b5 axb5 **3** f5 any, and White is stalemated.

51. 8128.

71. $4! + 5! + 7! = 24 + 120 + 5040 = (5^2 - 1) + (11^2 - 1) + (71^2 - 1) = 72^2$.

108. $325 = 1^2 + 18^2 = 6^2 + 17^2 = 10^2 + 15^2$.

34. White marbles can only be removed from the box in pairs. There is an odd number of white marbles to start with, so the last marble in the box will be white.

90. Other than rotations and reflections there is only one solution. The best way to start is with the central number, which must be a factor of 45, the sum of all nine numbers.

5	1	4
6	3	8
2	7	9

63. Anyone for tennis?

65. The players scored 5, 7, 11, 13, 17, 19, 29, 31, 37, 41, and 43 goals. Their average was 23 goals.

149. $71 = (4! + 4.4)/.4$

47. The solution to LAGER × 4 = REGAL is 21978 × 4 = 87912.

77. Sweet tooth.

129. Out of court.

139. **1** Qe6+ Kh8 **2** Nf7+ Kg8 **3** Nh6+ Kh8 **4** Qg8+ Rxg8 **5** Nf7 mate.

153. Bob up and down.

87. Four and three. The numbers are the numbers of letters in the words of the question.

24. To show the perimeter is divided into two equal lengths, whatever the angle of the arrow, let the diameter of each of the smaller semicircles (and thus the radius of the large semicircle) be d and let the arrow lie at an angle of a radians to the horizontal.

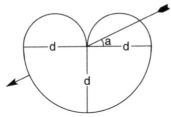

The perimeter length lying above the horizontal line is $^{\pi d}\!/_2 + {^{\pi d}\!/_2} = \pi d$, which is the perimeter length lying below the horizontal line. Therefore, to prove the heart's perimeter is divided into two equal lengths, we need to show that the part of the perimeter above the horizontal line and below the arrow is equal in length to the part of the perimeter that is below the horizontal line and above the arrow.

Begin by letting C be the center of the smaller semicircle on the right as shown below:

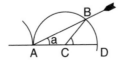

Since triangle ABC is isosceles, angle BCD is 2a radians. Thus the length of arc BD is $^{2a}\!/_{2\pi}$ multiplied by the perimeter of the small circle $= {^{2a}\!/_{2\pi}} \times \pi d = ad$. This is also the length of the arc of the big semicircle that is below the horizontal line and above the arrow and so the result is proven.

156. Lucky break.

60. Old is 30 and Young is 18.

107. Weeping willow.

101. Maverick, subtle (or bustle), pique, golfer, jinx, wrap, brazen, and holiday.

118. 3,782,915,460.

146. The pairs are:

$$^{355}/_{113} = 3.1415929... \quad (\pi = 3.1415926...)$$
$$^{577}/_{408} = 1.414215... \quad (\sqrt{2} = 1.414213...)$$
$$^{878}/_{323} = 2.71826... \quad (e = 2.71828...)$$
$$^{987}/_{610} = 1.618032... \quad (\phi = 1.618033...)$$

where π is the area of a circle of unit radius, e is the base for natural logarithms, and ϕ is the golden ratio. Interesting properties of ϕ include its relationship with its square (which equals $\phi + 1$) and its reciprocal (which equals $\phi - 1$). $\phi = (1 + \sqrt{5})/2$.

137. 916.

44. One step forward, two steps back.

83. The diagram contains 47 triangles in total, as below:

1 triangle of full size	6 triangles of ½ size
3 triangles of ⅓ size	10 triangles of ¼ size
6 triangles of ⅙ size	12 triangles of ⅛ size
3 triangles of 1/12 size	6 triangles of 1/24 size

13. Round of drinks on the house.

46. Reading between the lines.

161. The hands on the clock face show roughly when Heather left her room. The hour hand has moved $(x - 35)$ minutes since 7 P.M., and the minute hand y minutes. Since the minute hand moves twelve times faster than the hour hand, $y = 12(x - 35)$.

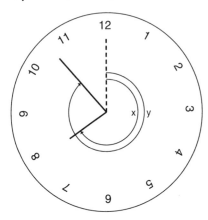

Now consider the position when the hands have changed places. The hour hand will have moved $(y - 50)$ minutes since 10 P.M., and the minute hand x minutes. Hence $x = 12(y - 50)$.

Solving these equations, $x = 39\frac{63}{143}$ and $y = 53\frac{41}{143}$. Thus the time elapsed since Heather left her room was 2 hours 46 minutes $9\frac{3}{13}$ seconds.

150. "We" are the number of letters in each word. Thus "twelve" is six, "nine" is four, etc.

113. 1 bxa8(N) Kxg2 2 Nb6 any 3 a8(B or Q) mate. Note that White's second move prevents 2 ... Bxa7.

138. The three names are Arnold, Roland, and Ronald.

9. 2,100,010,006.

166. Robin Hood.

133. Construct another regular five-pointed star as shown in the diagram. Since both are regular stars, $^{AB}/_{BC} = ^{AD}/_{DB}$.

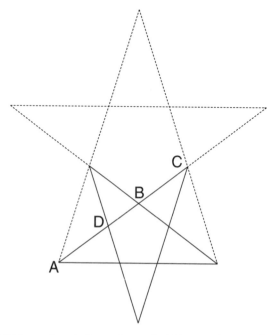

Let AB be of unit length and AD = BC = x (so DB = 1 − x). Then: $^{AB}/_{BC} = ^{AD}/_{DB}$ so $^1/_x = ^x/_{(1-x)}$.

So $x^2 + x - 1 = 0$, $x = -\frac{1}{2} + \frac{1}{2}\sqrt{5} = 0.618034$, and the ratio of AB to BC is the reciprocal of 0.618034, which is 1.618034.

41. A won against B, C, and D with scores of 3-0, 1-0, and 2-1 respectively. B won against C with a score of 1-0 and tied D with a score of 1-1. C won against D with a score of 2-0.

159. 1 d4 d5 2 Qd3 Qd6 3 Qh3 Qh6 4 Qxc8 mate.

67. Despite being the worst shot of the three, Arthur has the best chance of surviving, with a probability of .5222. Allwyn has the next best chance of surviving at .3 and Aitkins the least chance at .1778.

Arthur's tactic will be to aim to miss if the other two are alive. This is because the other two, if they get the choice, will fire at each other rather than Arthur. This will leave Arthur with the first shot at the survivor. The reason that Allwyn would choose to fire at Aitkins rather than Arthur is that he would rather have Arthur shooting at him with a 50% hit rate than Aitkins with an 80% success rate. The decision for Aitkins to fire at Allwyn rather than Arthur, if he gets the choice, is because for Aitkins to fire successfully at Arthur would be to sign his own death warrant.

72. By factorizing 2,450 and then compiling a list of the age groups with the desired product, it is found that only two have the same sum, namely 64. Thus Jim is 32, and the three passengers are either 50, 7, and 7 or 49, 10, and 5.

When he was told there was someone older than Bob on the bus, Jim was able to determine the passengers' ages. Obviously Bob cannot be older than 49, and if he were younger than this then both groups would still have been acceptable. Thus, knowing Bob was 49, Jim was able to determine the three passengers were aged 50, 7, and 7.

93. If this position had occurred in a real game, then Black's last move must have been g7-g5. Therefore, White can force mate in two with 1 hxg6 e.p. Kh5 2 Rxh7 mate.

85. Receding hairline.

86.

```
              6  6 . 3  7  5
    1  6 ) 1  0  6  2
              9  6
              1  0  2
                 9  6
                 6  0
                 4  8
                 1  2  0
                 1  1  2
                       8  0
                       8  0
```

127.

8	1	1	2	3	4	2
4	2	6	8	0	8	4
4	2	2	4	1	6	2
5	6	8	0	2	4	4
2	1	4	1	5	0	6
2	4	5	2	7	4	8
4	2	2	2	6	2	4

100. 18, since $18^3 = 5,832$ and $18^4 = 104,976$.

25. Bend over backwards.

163. The middle of nowhere.

84. $\sqrt{(6! + (6! + 6)/6)} = 29$.

14. 11, 47, and 71.

68. One foot in the grave.

79.

O			X		
			X		
		O			
	X		X		
			O	O	

115. At least two blocks are featured. The first five views are all consistent with each other, but the sixth is not. The "Z" on the upper face would have to be a "U" (with its base at the edge adjoining the face with the "E") for this block to match the others.

32. The traveler on the fast train sees all the trains going the other way around that left up to three hours ago or that will leave in the next two hours. The traveler on the slow train sees all the trains going the other way around that left up to two hours ago or that will leave in the next three hours. In five hours, including the beginning and end, 21 trains depart in each direction. Including the train they are traveling on, each traveler therefore sees 22 trains on his journey.

148. Split level.

36. There are 120 socks in the drawer: 85 red ones and 35 blue ones.

140. Construct the line CG as shown below:

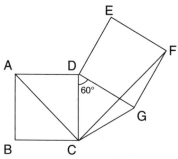

Since DC = DG and angle CDG is 60°, triangle CDG is equilateral, so DC = DG = CG.

Thus, triangle CGF is isosceles, since CG = GF. Angle CGF is angle CGD + angle DGF, which is 60° + 90°, or 150°. So angles GCF and GFC are both 15°.

Since angle DCG is 60° and angle GCF is 15°, angle FCD is 45°. Angle ACD is also 45°, so angle ACF is the sum of FCD and ACD, or 45° + 45°, which is 90°.

80. $6 / (1 - \frac{5}{7}) = 21$.

97. The two hands clearly cannot occur in the same deal, so we compare the number of hands that beat these two. They are both beaten by the same number of four-of-a-kinds, but the first hand is beaten by 32 straight flushes, the second by 31. Hence the full house with the three kings is the stronger hand.

158. Three wise men.

128. Five thousand.

114. Queueing.

49. Bermuda Triangle.

61.

69. The two possible ways of dividing the square are shown below:

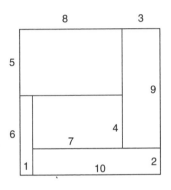
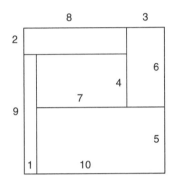

141. They are the same. Let $S = \sqrt{(12 + \sqrt{(12 + \sqrt{(12 + \sqrt{(12 + \ldots)})})})}$, then $S^2 = 12 + S$, from which $S = 4$. To evaluate $X = 2 + \sqrt{(2 + \sqrt{(2 + \sqrt{(2 + \ldots)})})}$, let $T = X - 2 = \sqrt{(2 + \sqrt{(2 + \sqrt{(2 + \ldots)})})}$. Then $T^2 = 2 + T$ from which $T = 2$ and $X = 4 = S$.

147. The four ages are 12, 16, 42, and 44.

37. 72 hens, 21 sheep, 7 cows.

89. Unfinished Symphony.

117. $123 - 45 - 67 + 89 = 100$.

48. This puzzle is designed so that most people who see it will think (falsely) that the clues are missing. They think this because they mistake the clues for clue numbers. The clues cannot be the clue numbers, however, since for one thing the puzzle would not then be solvable, and for another the order of the clues has been muddled up.

Clue 21-Across is 21 or, in letters, TWENTY-ONE. Once this clue has been solved the rest are easy. The answer is shown below:

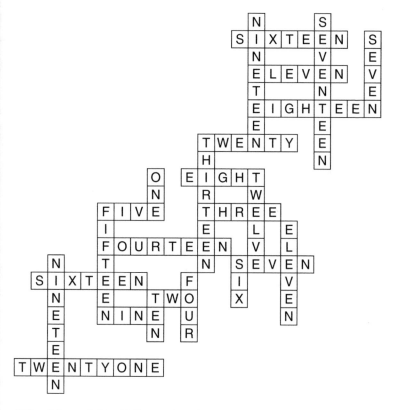

70. 93 and 87. When the digits in each number of the sequence are reversed, the sequence is the multiples of 13; that is, 13, 26, 39, 52, 65, 78, and 91.

119. Let the width of the star be 2a, and construct a line from the center of the star (and circle) to where one of the two outer threads meets the circle.

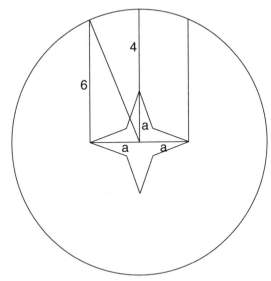

Clearly, the radius of the circle is 4 + a. The diagonal line is a radius, but it is also the hypotenuse of a right-angled triangle with sides of length 6 and a. Thus by the Pythagorean theorem we have $6^2 + a^2 = (4 + a)^2$, so a equals 2.5 cm and the width of the star is 5 cm.

109. The base n of the measurements can be found using the Pythagorean theorem, which gives the following decimal equation: $7^2 + (2n)^2 = (n + 3)^2 + (n + 8)^2$, from which n = 12. Thus the base being used in the question is 12, and using this base, the hypotenuse measures 21. In base ten the sides are 7, 24, and 25, and 15, 20, and 25.

162. I would not want a tiger to chase me or a zebra to chase me. Given the choice, I'd rather a tiger chased a zebra, not me.

15. TWELVE $= 130760$, THIRTY $= 194215$, and NINETY $= 848015$.

33.

C	D	X	C	I	V	D
L	V	M	M	I	I	L
X	C	I	X	D	X	V
I	C	C	X	C	I	I
C	M	L	X	X	I	X
X	I	I	I	V	C	I
I	X	X	X	I	I	I

64. Noting that the 3-5 domino can be placed uniquely, the full array is soon easily figured out, as shown.

1	2	6	1	6	3	4	5
3	3	6	4	3	2	5	4
3	0	6	0	3	1	2	2
0	5	5	4	6	5	0	2
0	2	5	1	5	0	0	1
6	4	3	4	4	1	1	1
2	2	6	4	5	0	3	6

155. There is no choice regarding the queen and king; each has only one square on which to be placed. The rooks, knights, and bishops can each be positioned in two ways, giving a total of $2^3 = 8$ different combinations. The eight pawns can be positioned in $8! = 40,320$ ways. Thus for the pieces of one color there are a total of $8 \times 40,320 = 322,560$ possibilities.

57. The integers are -3, -1, and 1.

26. The new chart is shown below:

Last week		This week	Last week		This week
Atomic	1	Atomic	Valentine	21	Another Day
Blockbuster	2	Dizzy	What	22	Kayleigh
Classic	3	Footloose	Xanadu	23	Xanadu
Dizzy	4	Blockbuster	YMCA	24	Angie Baby
Emma	5	Jesamine	Zabadak!	25	True
Footloose	6	Classic	Autumn Almanac	26	Mickey
Gaye	7	Night	Angie Baby	27	YMCA
Hello	8	Perfect	Another Day	28	Valentine
Intuition	9	Lamplight	Angel Eyes	29	Angel Eyes
Jesamine	10	Emma	Angel Fingers	30	Ain't Nobody
Kayleigh	11	What	Amateur Hour	31	Amateur Hour
Lamplight	12	Obsession	Angela Jones	32	New entry
Mickey	13	Autumn Almanac	Ain't Nobody	33	Angel Fingers
Night	14	Gaye	American Pie	34	Question
Obsession	15	Reward	Ant Rap	35	Always Yours
Perfect	16	Hello	Alphabet Street	36	Adoration Waltz
Question	17	American Pie	Alternate Title	37	Alternate Title
Reward	18	Intuition	As Usual	38	Sandy
Sandy	19	As Usual	Adoration Waltz	39	Alphabet Street
True	20	Zabadak!	Always Yours	40	Angela Jones

123.

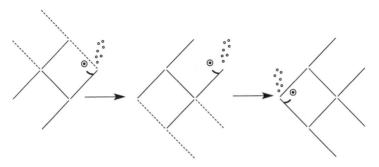

116. See-through blouse.

94.

3	6	1
5	2	9
7	8	4

73. Mate in three can be forced only by **1** d4.
If **1** ... Kh5 then **2** Qd3 Kg4 (or Kh4) **3** Qh3 mate.
If **1** ... Kg4 then **2** e4+ Kh4 **3** g3 mate.

130.

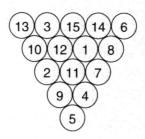

144. Let the longer candle burn at L $^{cm}/_{hr}$ and the shorter candle at S $^{cm}/_{hr}$. Then the longer candle was 8L cm, the shorter candle 8.75S cm, and 8L = 8.75S + 2.

At 8 P.M. the candles were the same length, so 4L = 5S. Solving with the above, S = ⅘ and L = 2, so the longer candle was 16 cm and the shorter candle was 14 cm.

124. Crossroads.

6. Square meal.

76. West Indies.

136. Too few to mention.

74. This is H.E. Dudeney's solution:

1	Nc3	d5
2	Nxd5	Nc6
3	Nxe7	g5
4	Nxc8	Nf6
5	Nxa7	Ne4
6	Nxc6	Nc3
7	Nxd8	Rg8
8	Nxf7	Rg6
9	Nxg5	Re6
10	Nxh7	Nb1
11	Nxf8	Ra3
12	Nxe6	b5
13	Nxc7+	Kf7
14	Nxb5	Kg6
15	Nxa3	Kh5
16	Nxb1	Kh4

22.

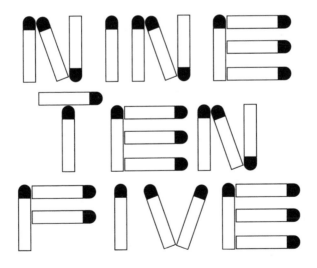

99. Space Invaders.

31. The minimum number of moves made by White's men to reach the position shown in the question is: queen's pawn 5 (d4, c5, b6, a7, a8), new queen 2 (a7, e3), queen's knight 2 (c3, a4), king's knight 2 (f3, h2), king's rook 2 (h3, g3), king's rook's pawn 2 (h3, g4), king's bishop's pawn 1 (f3) and king 1 (f2). These total seventeen and therefore account for all of White's moves. Noting that Black's missing pieces were captured on c5, b6, a7, and g4, the position after White's ninth move would have been as follows:

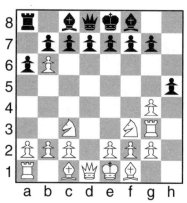

The game from White's ninth move was:

9 ...	Ra7
10 bxa7	h4
11 a8(Q)	h3
12 Qa7	h2
13 Qe3	h1(B)
14 Nh2	a5
15 f3	a4
16 Kf2	a3
17 Na4	

10. e^π is greater than π^e. To two decimal places, $e^\pi = 23.14$ and $\pi^e = 22.46$.

134. The values of A, B, and C are 1111, 2222, and 5555, respectively, and the question is whether $B^C + C^B$ is divisible by seven.

$B^C + C^B = (B^C + C^B) + (4^C - 4^B) - (4^C - 4^B)$
$= (B^C + 4^C) + (C^B - 4^B) - 4^B(64^A - 1^A)$

Since C is odd, $(B^C + 4^C)$ is divisible by $(B + 4)$, which is divisible by seven. $(C^B - 4^B)$ is divisible by $(C - 4)$, which is divisible by seven. Lastly, $4^B(64^A - 1^A)$ is divisible by $(64 - 1)$, which is divisible by seven. Thus $B^C + C^B$ is divisible by seven.

142. Laid back.

95. Digital Root $(9^{6130} + 2)^{4875}$
$\quad$ = Digital Root $(2^{4875} + 9 \times \text{(large number)})$
$\quad$ = Digital Root $(8^{1625} + 9)$
$\quad$ = Digital Root $((9 - 1)^{1625} + 9)$
$\quad$ = Digital Root $((9 \times \text{(large number)} - 1) + 9)$
$\quad$ = Digital Root $(9 - 1 + 9)$
$\quad$ = 8

12. By changing his mind, B reduced his chance of winning the game.

The only way in which EEE can appear before OEE is if the first three throws of the die are EEE. Otherwise the sequence EEE must be preceded by an O. The probability of the first three throws being E is $(\frac{1}{2})^3$, so if B chooses OEE when A has chosen EEE, then B wins with probability $\frac{7}{8}$. If B chooses OOO in response to A's choice of EEE, then B's chance of winning is $\frac{1}{2}$.

4. Each match will eliminate one player, so starting with 89 players will require 88 matches to decide the winner.

53. Just between you and me.

16. A straight-line route that takes the spider one meter down to the floor, forty meters across the floor, and nine meters up toward the ceiling is fifty meters.

Two quicker straight-line routes, found by drawing straight lines from the spider to the fly on a flattened plan of the warehouse, are shown below. The first of these sees the spider heading up the side wall, crossing the ceiling, and finally approaching the fly from above. The distance of this route is $\sqrt{(14^2 + 46^2)} = 48.08$ meters.

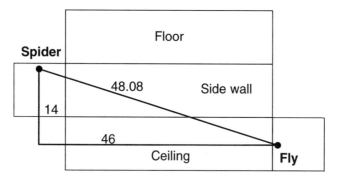

The third straight-line route sees the spider heading diagonally to the floor, then up the side wall, crossing the corner of the ceiling and again at the end approaching the fly from above. The distance of this route is $\sqrt{(20^2 + 42^2)} = 46.52$ meters.

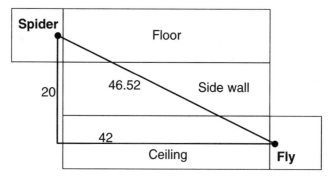

The shortest route is 46.52 meters.

29. The letter m.

50.

```
              1   4   5
2  0  6 ) 2   9   8   7   0
          2   0   6
              9   2   7
              8   2   4
              1   0   3   0
              1   0   3   0
```

Acknowledgments

Our thanks are due to many people, without whose help this book would not have been possible. To name but some:

• The London Staple Inn Actuarial Society, which publishes *The Actuary* and which published its predecessor, *Fiasco*. The vast majority of the puzzles in this book have previously been published in one of these magazines.

• To the editors of *The Actuary* and *Fiasco*, for their support and encouragement to us as puzzle editors.

• To those named in the book and those listed below (and we apologize if we have overlooked anyone) for creating or suggesting puzzles that we have used: 14–Heather Marshall, 30–David Walters, 33–Terry Wills, 55–Roger Gilbert, 60–L.J. Gray, 61–Steven Haberman, 62–K.J. Fagg, 65–Danny Roth, 69–Terry Wills, 72–John Sant, 80–Maurice Steinhart, 83–Paul McHugh, 101–David Twigger, 127–David Wharton, 150–H.E. Dudeney.

Index

Numbers refer to puzzle numbers.

The authors are always pleased to hear of new puzzles. If you have a puzzle that you think we could use in our next book, please send it to us with details on its source and your suggested solution. If we use your puzzle, we will acknowledge your contribution. Our e-mail addresses are timsole@xtra.co.nz and rodmarshall@enta.net.

What Is American Mensa?

American Mensa
The High IQ Society

One out of 50 people qualifies
for American Mensa …
Are YOU the One?

American Mensa, Ltd. is an organization for individuals who have one common trait: a score in the top two percent of the population on a standardized intelligence test. Over five million Americans are eligible for membership … you may be one of them.

• Looking for intellectual stimulation?
You'll find a good "mental workout" in the *Mensa Bulletin*, our national magazine. Voice your opinion in the newsletter published by your local group. And attend activities and gatherings with fascinating programs and engaging conversation.

• Looking for social interaction?
There's something happening on the Mensa calendar almost daily. These range from lectures to game nights to parties. Each year, there are over 40 regional gatherings and the Annual Gathering, where you can meet people, exchange ideas, and make interesting new friends.

• Looking for others who share your special interest? Whether your interest might be as common as computer gaming or as esoteric as eugenics, there's probably a Mensa Special Interest Group (SIG) for you. There are over 150 SIGs, which are started and maintained by members.

So contact us today to receive a free brochure and application.

American Mensa, Ltd.
1229 Corporate Drive West
Arlington, TX 76006
(800) 66-MENSA
AmericanMensa@compuserve.com
http://www.us.mensa.org

If you don't live in the U.S. and would like to get in touch with your national Mensa, contact:

Mensa International
15 The Ivories
6-8 Northampton Street, Islington
London N1 2HY England